A GUIDE FOR GRIEVING TEEN

Understanding and Helping Teens Heal From Grief

Victoria Fannie

INTRODUCTION

The teenage years are a period of progress. Bodies change. Sentiments change. Connections change. Teens pull back from their family to foster their own personalities. They seek after heartfelt connections and new interests. It's a difficult time that is made more troublesome when adolescents experience the passing of a huge adored one. While individuals of any age battle with misfortune, adolescent sorrow is especially complicated as they have a preferred comprehension of death over more younger children, yet may battle to discover approaches to offset their distress with their craving to find a place with their companions and discover freedom from their folks.

How teens grieve

Teenagers feel things profoundly, however frequently work to conceal those sentiments – especially from their family. It is significant that guardians and other caring grown-ups assisting teens with managing anguish know about the inconspicuous indications of despondency in a teenager. These signs can include:

-Absence of focus

-Outrage

-Self-fault

-Irritability

-Anxiety

-Lower grades

-Loss of interest in common exercises

-Over-action (accomplishing more homework, additional tasks, anything to shut out contemplations of the misfortune)

-Needing to be distant from everyone else more

-Eating excessively or excessively little

-Use or maltreatment of drugs or alcohol

-Sleep deprivation or dozing more than expected

-Self-hurt

-Risk-taking conduct

-Self-destructive ideation

CHAPTER ONE

Helping grieving teen

Regardless of whether a teen has encountered misfortune previously, this might be whenever they're originally expected to completely take an interest in a burial service or opposite finish of-life customs. Families can begin assisting a teen manage sadness by setting them up for what's in store. Not knowing what the legitimate manners is for the occasion can cause added uneasiness for teens who don't have the foggiest idea what's in store or the proper behavior. Families can likewise include them in the arranging of the administrations and inquire as to whether they might want to be a piece of the assistance in any capacity. They can urge a grieving youngster to take part in the administrations, yet ought not to drive them.

Tell teens that misery doesn't end with the burial service or commemoration administration. From multiple points of view, this is only the start of the pain recuperation measure. Tell grieving teens that it can assist with communicating their sentiments and praise the individual they have lost.

Talking to your teens about grief

Instructions to Converse with teens about grief: It is consistently agonizing when a friend or family member passes on. Adults can assist teens with managing sorrow by sharing their own sentiments about the misfortune and discussing a portion of the clashing feelings they might feel. They can tell teens that every individual's sadness is interesting and that it doesn't follow a direct way. They might be glad for quite a long time and afterward experience an enthusiastic mishap. This is typical.

Discovering approaches to celebrate and respect the individual they have lost is a decent method to assist teens with preparing melancholy and make them talk. Families can make a scrapbook or shadowbox with prized recollections. Different thoughts remember establishing a tree for their adored one's memory or lighting a memorable flame them.

Families should tell grieving teens that proficient mourning help is accessible. Teenagers might oppose finding support right away. It's typical for teenagers to excuse advising a few times prior to consenting to attempt it. A joint first meeting can be a decent method to begin to assist them with slipping into the thought. On the off chance that the teen keeps on opposing, the family should converse with a grief instructor about alternate approaches to help them.

Children and teens express their anguish in an assortment of ways. Some might be tragic and express the misfortune like numerous grown-ups. Contingent upon their ages, be that as it may, they might show pity just some of the time and for brief periods. Children might whine of actual inconvenience, like stomachaches or migraines. Or then again they might communicate nervousness or misery about different difficulties, like everyday schedule.

Misfortune is more extreme when the youngster had a cozy relationship with the individual who passed on, like a parent or kin. In any case, this isn't generally clear from a kid's responses. A child's sorrow might appear to go back and forth. Also, a kid may once in a while verbally express their misery. This is ordinary. Your child may likewise re-experience the force of the misfortune as the individual in question grows up. This might happen all the more frequently during specific achievements throughout everyday life, like beginning everyday schedule on a first date. Indeed, even into adulthood, significant occasions, for example, moving on from school or getting hitched may trigger restored grief.

Understanding how teens view death

It is useful to know how children comprehend death at various phases of improvement. It shifts by age and regularly changes as a child grows sincerely and socially. Different factors additionally impact children's responses. These can incorporate character, past encounters with death, and backing from relatives. Remember that youngsters don't move unexpectedly from 1 phase of improvement to the following. Furthermore, highlights from each stage might cover.

-Newborn children (birth to 2 years: Have no comprehension of death.

Know about detachment and will lament the shortfall of a parent or guardian.

May respond to the shortfall of a parent or guardian with expanded crying, diminished responsiveness, and changes in eating or resting.

May continue looking or requesting a missing guardian or parental figure and sit tight for that person to return.

Are generally influenced by the trouble of enduring parent(s) and guardians.

-Preschool-age children (3 to 6 years): Are interested with regards to death and trust it is brief or reversible.

May consider passing to be something like resting. All in all, the individual is dead yet just limitedly and may keep on breathing or eat in the afterlife.

Regularly feel remorseful and accept that they are answerable for the demise of a friend or family member, maybe in light of the fact that they were "terrible" or wished the individual would "disappear."

May feel that they can make the individual who kicked the bucket return in case they are adequate.

May stress over who will deal with them and about being abandoned.

Are extremely influenced by the misery of enduring relatives.

Can't adequately articulate their sentiments and on second thought respond to misfortune through practices like touchiness, hostility, actual manifestations, trouble resting, or relapse, (for example, bed-wetting or thumb-sucking).

-School-age children (6 to 12 years)

Comprehend that demise is conclusive.

May consider demise an individual or a soul, similar to a phantom, heavenly messenger, or a skeleton.

By age 10, comprehend that death happens to everybody and can't be stayed away from. Are regularly intrigued by the particular subtleties of death and what befalls the body in the afterlife.

May encounter a scope of feelings including culpability, outrage, disgrace, tension, bitterness, and stress over their own passing.

Battle to discuss their sentiments. Their sentiments might come out through practices, for example, school evasion, lackluster showing in school, hostility, actual manifestations, withdrawal from friends, and relapse.

May stress over who will deal with them, and will probably encounter sensations of uncertainty, tenacity, and deserting?

May stress that they are to be faulted for the passing.

Teenagers (13 to 18 years)

Have a grown-up comprehension of the idea of death yet don't have the encounters, adapting abilities, or conduct of a grown-up.

May carry on out of frustration at relatives or show imprudent or wild practices, for example, substance use, battling in school, and sexual indiscrimination.

May encounter a wide scope of feelings yet not realize how to deal with them or not feel open to discussing them.

May scrutinize their confidence or their comprehension of the world.

May not be responsive to help from grown-up relatives due to be autonomous and separate from guardians.

May adapt by investing more energy with companions or by pulling out from the family to be separated from everyone else.

CHAPTER TWO

Helping your teen cope with loss of loved one

Clarify demise in basic, immediate, genuine terms outfitted to your kid's formative level. Kids can't consider their considerations and feelings like grown-ups. So they should have many short discussions. Grown-ups may have to rehash a similar data commonly. Children might pose similar inquiries regularly as they attempt to figure out troublesome data.

Tips to help explain death and loss to your child

Clarify passing utilizing genuine words, for example, "kicked the bucket" instead of befuddling expressions, for example, "rested."

You can say that demise implies the individual's body has quit working or that the individual can at this point don't inhale, talk, move, eat, or any of the things the person could do when alive.

Offer your family's spiritual beliefs about death or profound.

Urge your child to pose inquiries, and attempt to answer them sincerely and straightforwardly. In the event that you don't have a clue about the response to an inquiry, assist with discovering the appropriate response.

Use books, drawings, or pretend games to assist a younger child with getting death.

Here are ideas that might help your child adapt to a loss:

-Ensure your child comprehends that the individual isn't at fault for the death and that the individual who died on isn't returning.

-Give bunches of friendship and console your kid frequently that the individual in question will keep on being cherished and really focused on.

-Urge your child to discuss their feelings. Recommend alternate approaches to communicate sentiments, like writing in a diary or drawing an image.

-Without overpowering your child, share your misery with that person. Communicating your feelings can empower your child or little girl to share their own feelings.

-Assist your child with understanding that typical sorrow includes a scope of feelings, including outrage, responsibility, and disappointment. Clarify that their feelings and responses might be totally different from those of adults.

-Promise your child that it is typical for the aggravation of distress to travel every which way after some time. Clarify that they can't generally anticipate when they will feel miserable.

-In the event that your kid is more seasoned, urge the person in question to converse with an adult external the family, like an educator or a pastorate part. You can likewise consider an age-explicit care group.

-Keep schedules and parental figures as steady as could really be expected, and keep drawing certain lines on conduct. Care, consistency, and congruity assist children with having a sense of security.

-Energize investing energy with companions and participating in other age-suitable exercises.

-Promise your child that it is never unfaithful to the individual who died to feel glad and to have a great time.

-Talk with a sadness guide, child therapist, or other psychological well-being proficient in case you are worried about your child's conduct.

-Tending to every day schedule and job changes

The death of a parent or other close relative can straightforwardly influence a kid's everyday life. Family schedules and jobs change, for example, an enduring guardian getting back to work and invest less energy at home. These progressions are an additional disturbance and may add to a child's trouble. Indeed, even little children will profit from additional arrangement, discussions, and backing around these changes.

Although the death of a relative with disease is agonizing, it might likewise diminish a portion of a kid's pressure. For instance, the passing of a kin may imply that a parent isn't splitting time between a debilitated kid at the clinic and one more kid at home. It is ordinary to have solid, blended sentiments, including some alleviation, when a relative's enduring is over after a long or troublesome ailment. Assist your child with understanding that these sentiments are typical and that the individual ought not to feel regretful for having them.

Respecting and remembering the loved one who just passed on

Children as young as age 3 comprehend the idea of bidding farewell. They ought to be permitted to pick how they bid farewell to a friend or family member.

Give preschool-age and more seasoned children the decision of going to commemoration administrations. In any case, don't compel them to join in the event that they would prefer not to.

Some children might need to go to a remembrance administration however not a survey or internment.

Permit more seasoned kids and teens to assist with arranging dedications assuming they need.

Talk with youngsters regarding what will occur at an assistance early. Think about visiting the congregation or graveyard.

Request that a believed grown-up assist take with minding of little youngsters at a help or to return home with a kid who chooses the individual needs to leave early.

Assist your child with understanding that the individual who died lives on in their memory. Parents who are at death's door once in a while leave letters, recordings, or photos to assist youngsters with recalling the amount they were cherished. Children can likewise gather pictures and other exceptional things to make their own memory. For more young children, a large portion of their insight into the individual who passed on will come from recollections of other relatives. Talk about the individual frequently, and help kids to remember how much the expired individual adored them. Over the long run, children can comprehend that they would not be who they are without the impact of the unique individual who died.

CHAPTER THREE

UNDERSTANDING TEENGERS GRIEF: Helping tens deal with grief

It's hard to summarize how to help a child or teen without being excessively broad in light of the fact that, actually like large wrinkly people, they are convoluted people who think, feel, act, and respond to life in their own extraordinary manners.

A young adult's pain can be affected by quite a few things including yet not restricted to, their remarkable relationship with the individual, how the individual passed on, and their emotionally supportive network, past encounters with death, and their own novel qualities and shortcomings with regards to managing pressure, difficulty, and high feeling. Adults looking to help a teen should attempt to recall that a wide scope of reactions are considered 'ordinary' and there's nobody recipe for offering help.

Luckily, tried and true way of thinking says the most ideal approach to help a grieving teen is to 'partner' them, which is only an extravagant method of saying be there for them which you (ideally) definitely realize how to do. You can 'partner' a child by supporting them, talking straightforwardly and truly, tuning in, permitting them to lament how they need, and permitting them to choose how they will adapt (except for reckless practices).

No doubt I know, this sounds a ton like supporting grown-ups. What's more, although more young tweens teenagers actually have some work to do sincerely and formatively, more established adolescents (roughly 16-18) who can comprehend complex connections and other's perspectives, are probably going to lament similarly grown-ups do.

We instruct for teens with respect to any age you do the accompanying:

-Recognize their essence, their significance, their viewpoints, musings, and sentiments.

-Be patient and receptive. Permit them to lament in their own specific manner.

-Be accessible – Sit with the kid, pay attention to them, and answer their inquiries.

-Tell them that a scope of various feelings is typical.

-Approve their sentiments and don't limit them.

-Check in with different grown-ups engaged with their life – instructors, school guides, and mentors.

-Discover age-fitting assets. Look at our number one assets for supporting adolescents and young adults here.

Presently, I realize any individual who's consistently lived with a young adult is thinking,

"Buddy, I'm personally familiar with a child and they are nothing similar to adults."

Furthermore, you're correct, we would be delinquent in the event that we didn't recognize teens accompany their own arrangement of grief contemplations. Yet, accentuate the above on the grounds that toward the day's end our best counsel will consistently be to stroll with the teen through their pain while as yet regarding adult obligations like drawing limits, giving direction, and setting a genuine model. Alright so back to those teen despondency contemplations, when supporting a juvenile one ought to recollect the accompanying:

This might be their first involvement in death:

For some children, this is their first involvement in death. For critical connections, children might come to characterize their lives as far as 'before' the passing and 'after' the demise. After a demise, teen might encounter the accompanying interestingly:

End of life ceremonies and etiquette: Numerous children presently can't seem to go to a burial service or dedication administration a ways into their adolescent years. Ceremonies and behavior might cause uneasiness for young people, particularly on the off chance that they don't have a clue what's in store or acceptable behavior. Moreover, adolescents might be awkward with the sensation of being in front of an audience as everybody watches to perceive how they're adapting.

Tip: Set up the youngster for what's in store contingent upon the sort of administrations you will have. Remember them for the arranging. Talk regarding what, assuming any, components they might want to be a piece of and what, assuming any, they can quit. Urge them to partake yet don't constrain.

Feelings: For teenagers who have little involvement in injury, demise, agony, or stress, this will be whenever they first experience the mind-boggling feelings identified with anguish. This can be startling and many don't have the mindfulness to realize what sorts of adapting procedures will help. More on feelings later.

Tip: Standardize the scope of feelings mourners are able to encounter. Set them up for shifts in feeling and allow them to snicker and feel glad when they feel like it. Assist them with conceptualizing adapting systems dependent on their character and qualities. Offer choices like guiding, journaling, and exercise manuals, however don't push.

Inquiries concerning life's importance: Not all youngsters are prepared to consider life's mind boggling existential inquiries, however they are absolutely mature enough to examine 'why's and 'what for notwithstanding a passing. This might be the initial time their perspective, strict perspectives, or feeling of interminability has been tested.

Tip: Take into account open discourse about a daily existence's philosophical, religious, and strategic inquiries. Try not to limit their inquiries and assist them with tracking down their own replies. Backing them in conversing with strict pioneers if fitting. Attempt to recollect that while you've had a very long time to consider the importance of life and demise, these are questions they are just barely starting to inquire.

CHAPTER FOUR

Coping skills

Most teens are reliant upon adults or potentially their relatives for something. A demise in the essential emotionally supportive network can cause tension and stress for children on the grounds that there's the potential for things like family structures, living plans, funds, enthusiastic help, and everyday living to change. A passing can debilitate the essential emotionally supportive network/family structure in the accompanying ways:

Loss of a parent: The demise of a parent can gigantically affect a youngster. Duh. OK, so which parent passed on? Was it their sexual orientation good example? Was it the parent who they depended on the most? The slave driver? The blanket? The nurturer?

Tip: Consider the jobs this parent filled for the child and recognize these misfortunes. You can't supplant the parent, yet you might need to step in and fill their shoes somewhat. You may turn into the standard implementer or you should attempt to be to a greater degree a blanket (in your own specific manner kindly, don't be abnormal).

On the off chance that the expired was their equivalent sex parent, ponder other male/female grown-ups who could impact them. Invest more energy with that individual as a Crying girl family, or backing the youngster in investing one-on-one time with them (Accommodating Clue: Hint the grown-up in that they 'have been chosen', may the chances be ever in support of themselves).

Actual precariousness and instability: With the passing of a relative, actual steadiness can be compromised severally. A couple of models incorporate loss of monetary security, an adjustment of lodging, another school, or dread of being stranded.

Tip: Talk about the family's status, choices, and plans for the future with young people. Come clean with them and give them decisions, this will assist them with recapturing a feeling of control. A few changes can't be forestalled, so hold a family gathering to examine concerns and choose how predicaments can be made simpler.

Adult emotional instability: Following passing, teenagers might observer the grown-ups in control truly battle. Lamenting guardians and guardians might present as very enthusiastic, unfit to really focus on the teen's requirements, or incapable to fill parental jobs (maybe their own or maybe those of a perished parent).

Tip: It's alright to lament and show feeling before a young adult, this standardizes sentiments and sets a genuine model for communicating one's thoughts. Yet, act naturally mindful, if your feeling is outrageous it could cause tension for the juvenile as well as placed them in the situation of supporting you. In the event that you feel yourself letting completely go, it's an ideal opportunity to take a gander at your own adapting.

Parental discord: Sadness can strain connections, regardless of whether the demise just influences one-half of the couple. Because of pain guardians might pull out from each other, contend, get their sentiments injured, and additionally separate/separate. Intricacies in a relationship can significantly affect the child.

Tip: Families encountering outrageous friction should seriously think about seeing a Couples Specialist or a Marriage and Family Advisor. On the off chance that separation/separate is unavoidable, know this accompanies its own arrangement of inconveniences for a young adult and will perhaps feel like an optional misfortune.

They have their entire lives in front of them:

Which implies they have a day to day existence loaded with achievements and customs like weddings, graduations, figuring out how to drive, birthday celebrations, and first positions; and they probably envisioned their cherished one would be a piece of these. It's normal for youngsters to lament these future transitional experiences and afterward feel the misfortune once more when they happen.

Tip: When these occasions roll around, recognize the effect of the expired individual's nonappearance. Let the teen (or by then, at that point, grown-up) realize it's OK to feel pity despite the fact that it's likewise a cheerful day. Examine and urge imaginative approaches to join your cherished one's memory in the day/occasion. Look at our posts on recollecting your adored one on your big day here and here.

They're looking for their personality:

A significant assignment during childhood is simply the mission to characterize. What are their preferences? What are they acceptable at? What is their own style? What are their qualities and convictions? Unavoidably, as it does with everybody, the demise of somebody they love will affect how they characterize themselves in the present and future. Think about the accompanying:

They are the child whose [insert relation] kicked the bucket: It's normal for a youngster to be the main individual in their companion gathering to have encountered the demise of somebody significant. All things considered, they might feel alone they would say as well as like a curiosity to children who are ignorant regarding pain and death.

Tip: Be accessible to discuss their encounters. Try not to misinterpret it in the event that they attempt to disregard the misfortune and carry on as though nothing has occurred. To youngsters, peer connections can feel more significant than grown-up connections so they might like to converse with confided in companions as opposed to grown-ups. Offer them the chance to invest energy with different teenagers who've had comparable encounters through teen support gatherings or adolescent distress camps.

Do they need to take on new jobs because of the death? A lamenting adolescent might discover they need to help more around the house, particularly when their parent(s) are additionally lamenting. Children are frequently approached to take on grown-up obligations like carpooling, childcare, enthusiastic help, low maintenance occupations, and good example for more youthful kids.

Tip: Attempt to recollect that more youthful and center adolescents are not yet grown-ups. Truly investigate the fittingness of the jobs they're taking on. Obligation is great as long as it's age-fitting they actually possess satisfactory energy for the everyday schedule, and fun.

They can feel eclipsed by a kin's demise: Kids who've encountered the passing of a kin might wind up feeling disregarded and dominated. We urge guardians to discuss and recollect their perished kids; simply know that when the expired kid gets most of the consideration, living kin can feel desirous and stressed they don't have the right stuff.

Tip: Don't come close. It's in every case a word of wisdom to zero in on individual youngsters and their singular qualities. Ensure your kids stand out enough to be noticed and recognize their characteristics and achievements sooner rather than later... I mean, what difference would it make?

They might cover feeling or passionate articulations might appear to be unique:

Children experience and express feelings uniquely in contrast to grown-ups. Once more, duh. Your child's enthusiastic articulations might astonish you, they might appear to be over emotional or on the other hand they might appear to be quelled. Where feelings are concerned adolescents:

Might be humiliated with regards to their sentiments: Frequently, teenagers need to fit in and go unrecognized. 'Lamenting' may separate them in a manner they're not happy with. More young children particularly (12-14) will in general feel there is something of a nonexistent crowd watching what they do; thus, they might be mindful with regards to how and when they miserable boy express feelings. Teenagers, actually like grown-ups, may decide to lament secretly and may make light of their sorrow within the sight of others.

Tip: Permit the teenager to communicate their feelings when and how they like. Try not to cause them to feel regretful for going about like everything seems OK, this doesn't mean they couldn't care less. In case they're available to your help, assist them with discovering approaches to lament they're OK with. A few youths might discover solace in the security of a diary, book, or a one-on-one despondency guide. As usual, be patient and take cues from them.

Articulation of feeling might appear to be unstable: teens can move temperaments pretty quickly; brief they're glad and the following moment they're upset. Somewhat, these changes in mind-set are because of expanded chemicals and their creating cerebrums and bodies; yet the outrageous feelings of anguish can have the emotional episode impact on youngsters and grown-ups the same. You might wind up scratching your head considering what made them so agitated, however they may not have the option to distinguish the trigger (very much like adults).

Tip: Attempt to place their passionate articulation into setting. Comprehend the wide scope of feelings related with despondency and expect teenagers might be bound to communicate feelings like outrage than misery. Attempt to be open, tolerating, and approving of their feelings and ensure they know you're free to talk. Look for outside help in case you're stressed they've been bothered, removed, discouraged, or ruinous for a delayed timeframe. Look at our post on ordinary versus not really typical sorrow.

May appear to be self-centered: Young people, as a general rule, can be exceptionally self-centered. More youthful teenagers particularly (12-14) struggle considering other's points of view. This is an expertise that must be mastered as their cerebrum creates thus they regularly fall off looking narcissistic and ailing in sympathy. It follows that more youthful youngsters will experience issues understanding other's pain responses when they are unique in relation to their own. Jill's things are essential to me, how is it possible that Dad would tidy up out her room? I'm as yet pitiful, how is it possible that Mom would conceivably ponder dating?

Tip: Show restraint.

Youngsters are strong heroes (in their brain) for example imprudent insane individuals:

As a rule, teens are undeniably more hasty and ready to face challenges than their grown-up overseers. More youthful to center teenagers are particularly adept to feel powerful and undying. The two teenagers and adults utilize dangerous ways of dealing with stress like liquor, substance use, sex, reserved conduct, and pull out, yet children are less similar to liable to precisely survey hazard and utilize trustworthiness. On the other hand, they are bound to trial and take risky risks.

Tip: Here and there when a child encounters the unfathomable aggravation of melancholy, adults feel constrained to back off of them in manners that are excessively reasonable and empowering. Some of the time adults are excessively occupied by their own sorrow to see what's new with their children. Try not to allow this to occur – don't spare a moment to pose inquiries and award when it appears to be essential. Keep in mind, as a parent, guardian, or concerned grown-up you must define boundaries and put down certain boundaries. You will not have control of them for any longer, so put down certain boundaries while you can.

www.ingramcontent.com/pod-product-compliance
Ingram Content Group UK Ltd.
Pitfield, Milton Keynes, MK11 3LW, UK
UKHW022008190726
13853UKWH00004B/1812

9 798484 528394